Flowchart Science

The SKELETON AND MUSCLES

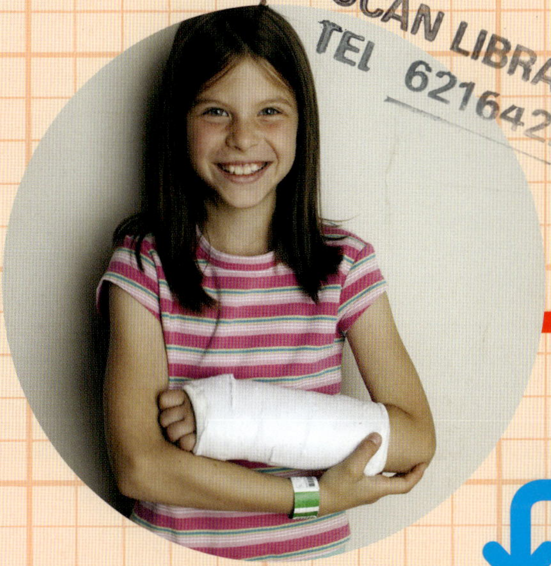

Richard and Louise Spilsbury

raintree
a Capstone company — publishers for children

Raintree is an imprint of Capstone Global Library Limited, a company incorporated in England and Wales having its registered office at 264 Banbury Road, Oxford, OX2 7DY – Registered company number: 6695582

www.raintree.co.uk
myorders@raintree.co.uk

Produced for Raintree by Calcium
Editors: Sarah Eason and Harriet McGregor
Designers: Paul Myerscough and Simon Borrough
Picture researcher: Rachel Blount
Originated by Capstone Global Library Limited © 2018

ISBN 978 1 4747 6583 1 (hardback)
22 21 20 19 18
10 9 8 7 6 5 4 3 2 1

ISBN 978 1 4747 6598 5 (paperback)
23 22 21 20 19
10 9 8 7 6 5 4 3 2 1

British Library Cataloguing in Publication Data
A full catalogue record for this book is available from the British Library.

Acknowledgements:
Cover art: Shutterstock: Boogie Man.
Picture credits: Shutterstock: Alenavlad 32–33, Potapov Alexander 12l, Ase 24c, Galina Barskaya 44–45, Business Stock 7r, Rommel Canlas 4–5, Neale Cousland 17b, Denk Creative 28, Dirima 31, Fizkes 6–7, Ganibal 9, Gelpi 11, Brian Goff 36, Fer Gregory 4b, Ifong 38, Iofoto 18, Sebastian Kaulitzki 19, 22–23, 34, Igor Kisselev 1, 13br, Lineartestpilot 14, Maridav 26–27, Stephen McSweeny 44l, Mls-e 32, Natursports 35, Nejron Photo 16–17, NoPainNoGain 30, Alena Ozerova 39, Todd Pettibone 27r, A. Ricardo 22b, Sudowoodo 43, Syda Productions 24–25, Vadimmmus 20, VectorLifestylepic 41b, Richard Whitcombe 12–13, YanLev 40–41, Yoko Design 10l.

Printed and bound in China.

Contents

Chapter 1

Amazing bones

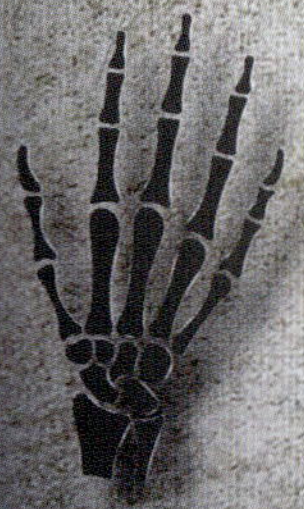

The bones inside the human body do an incredible and very important job. Together, the hard, white bones form the framework that holds the body up. This is the skeleton.

An adult human skeleton is made up of 206 bones that come in many shapes and sizes. The skull is the hard round bone that surrounds the **brain**. At the neck, the skull attaches to the **spine** (backbone). This is made up of 26 bones called **vertebrae** that are shaped like rings. The ribs give the chest its cage shape and the **pelvis**, which connects the spine to the legs, is shaped a little like a butterfly.

Different bones in the skeleton support the human body in different ways. Bones support the skin that covers the body, and gives humans their shape. The spine runs down the centre of the back and holds the body and head upright. It supports the upper parts of the body. As well as giving the body its shape and structure, the skeleton works together with the muscles inside the body to help us move.

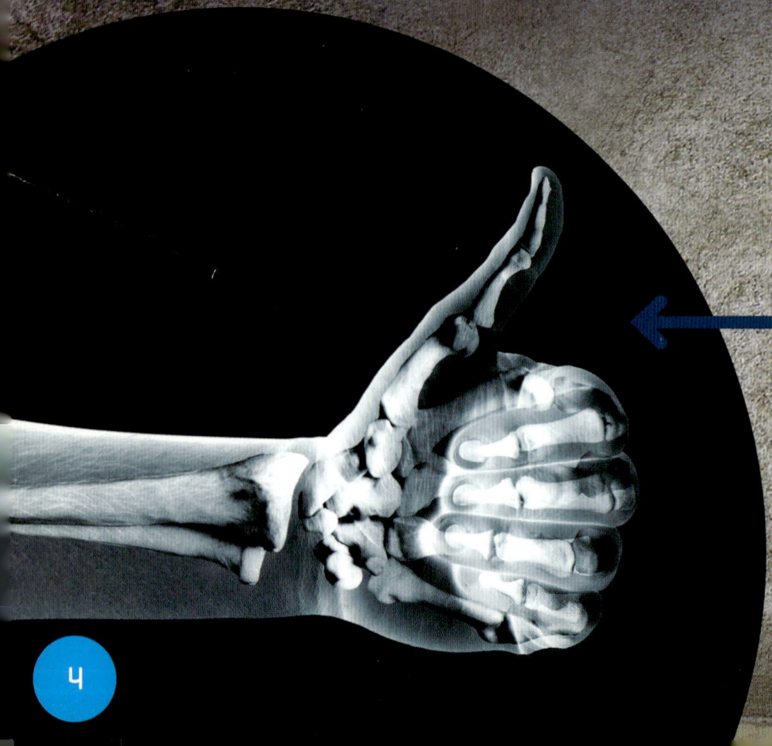

This x-ray shows the bones inside the arm. The white areas are the most dense.

Without its skeleton to hold it up, the human body would be as floppy as a jellyfish.

Get smart!

Doctors can see bones inside the body when they take x-ray images. X-rays are special rays of light that can pass through clothes and flesh but not through hard substances such as bone. An x-ray shows the bones inside the body as white shapes.

Bones and muscles

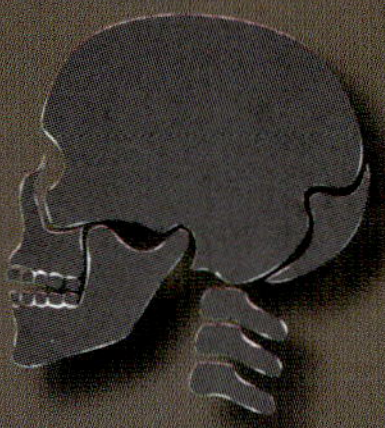

The bones that make up the body's skeleton cannot move by themselves. Bones only move because they are attached to muscles. The muscles pull on the bones and make them move. Most of the movements humans make use many muscles at the same time.

Muscles are masses of tough, elastic **tissue**. The human body has more than 600 muscles and these muscles make up half the body's weight. There are different types of muscles and they have a range of jobs. When we smile and talk, muscles help us communicate. Muscles move arms and legs, and even when people are not moving, some muscles are still working. Muscles make the heart beat, the chest rise and fall as people breathe, and blood flow through the body.

Muscles that move bones mostly only work when they are "told" to. When someone approaches a door, they see the handle and their eyes send this information to the brain. The brain sends a message back to tell the hand to open the door. The brain sends this message through **nerves** to the muscles in the arm. The message tells the muscles in the arm, hand and fingers to lift, move, grip and turn the door handle.

Some gymnastic moves, such as this one, require a combination of different, strong muscles in action at the same time.

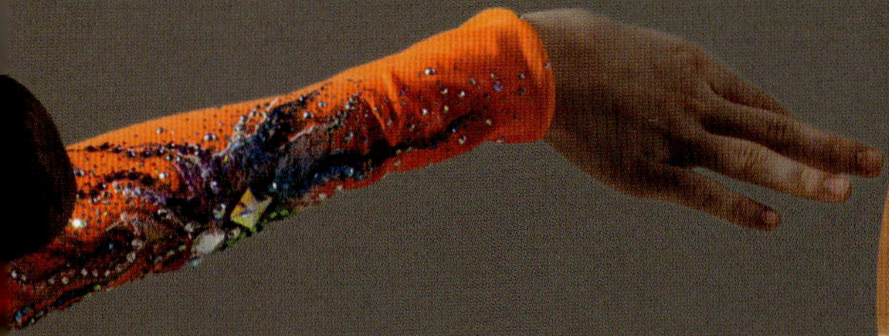

There are more than 30 individual muscles in the hand and forearm.

Get smart!

Bones are fastened to other bones by long, fibrous straps called ligaments. Ligaments are thick bands of stretchy tissue that work like elastic bands. They are strong enough to hold the bones in position as well as allowing them to move when muscles pull on the bones.

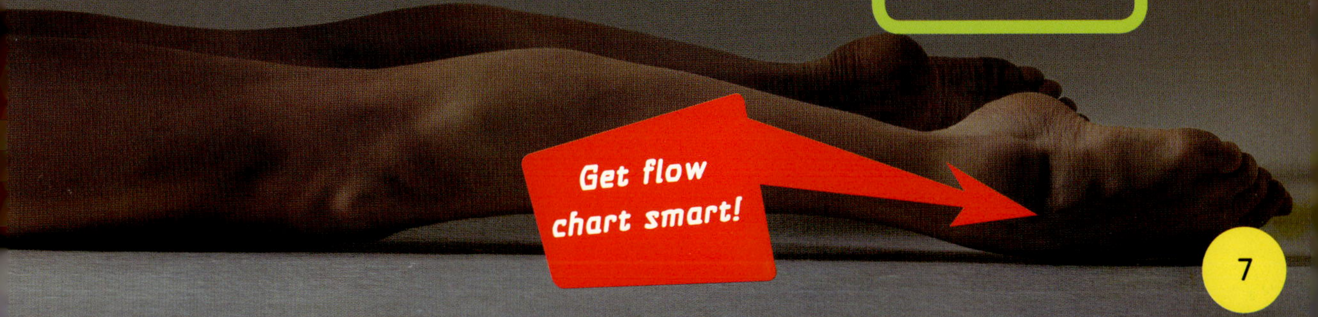

Get flow chart smart!

How bones move

Follow the steps in this flow chart to find out which processes are involved in a simple action.

A person sees a cup.

Nerves carry messages into the hand to tell muscles controlling the bones in the fingers to move and grip the cup.

Arm muscles move the cup towards the person's mouth so they can drink from it.

The eyes send a message to the brain that the cup is there.

The brain decides the person wants a drink and sends messages to the hand telling it to pick up the cup.

Messages travel from the brain, via nerves in the **spinal cord**, to the arm muscles to make the bones in the arm move towards the cup.

Flowchart Smart

Chapter 2
What are bones made of?

Bones are made mostly of a substance called **collagen**, which provides a soft framework, and **minerals**, such as **calcium**, which add strength and harden the framework. The bones that make up the human skeleton begin to develop when a baby is inside its mother, but they change as children grow.

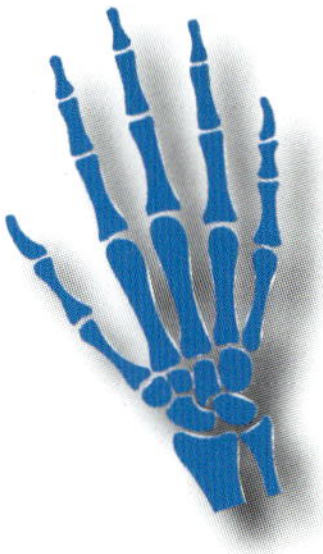

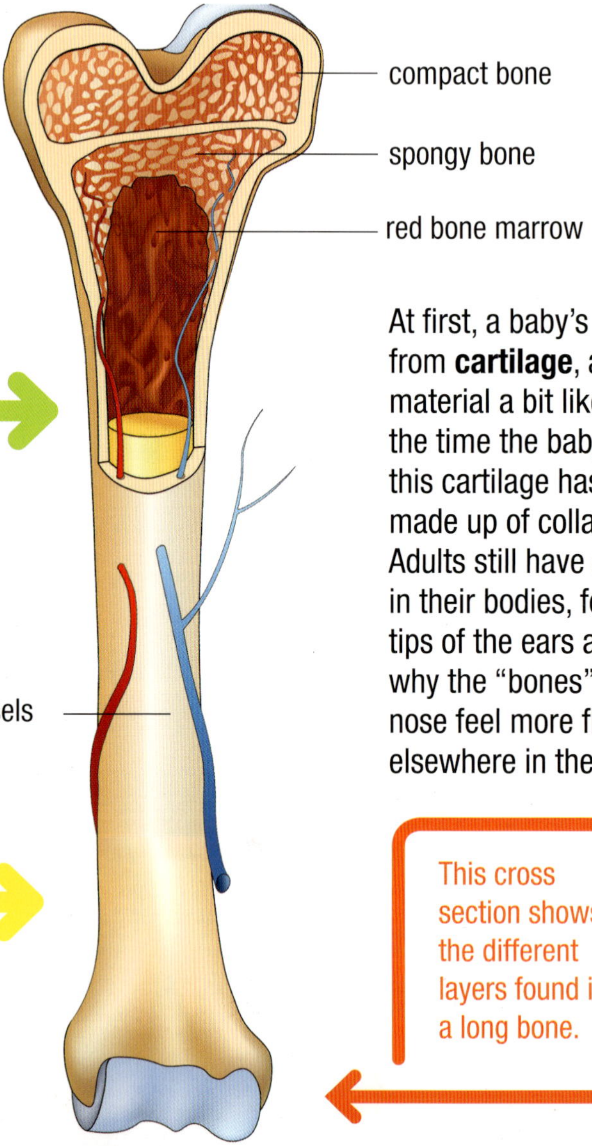

At first, a baby's skeleton is made from **cartilage**, a tough rubbery material a bit like soft bone. By the time the baby is born, most of this cartilage has turned into bone, made up of collagen and calcium. Adults still have some cartilage left in their bodies, for example, in the tips of the ears and nose. That is why the "bones" in the end of the nose feel more flexible than bones elsewhere in the body.

This cross section shows the different layers found in a long bone.

Bones are a combination of hard substances and living **cells**. The thick outer layer of the bone is compact bone. This is smooth, hard bone. It forms the structure of the bone and helps protect the more fragile layers inside. Spongy bone is found mostly at the ends of bones and joints. Spongy bone protects the bone marrow in the centre of the bone. Bone marrow looks a bit like thick jelly and it makes new blood cells for the rest of the body. **Nerves** and **blood vessels** are also present in bones. Blood vessels bring food and **oxygen** to bones so they can live and grow.

When a baby is born it has about 300 bones. As bones grow, some of these fuse together so that by the time a child becomes an adult it has a total of only 206 bones.

Get smart!

A baby's kneecaps are made from cartilage until the child is at least three years old. That is because very young children fall down a lot as they learn to walk. Cartilage is spongy and more flexible so is less likely to break. By the time a child is five years old, the cartilage will have turned into kneecaps of real bone.

Strong and tough

For its weight, bone is stronger than steel! Bones must be tough and strong because they support the weight of the human body in all the activities it does. Bones are also strong and tough because they must protect the body's precious organs.

The bones form a hard, protective covering over the inside parts of the body. The skull protects the brain. The bones that form the rib cage protect the heart, which pumps blood around the body. The rib bones also protect the lungs, the organs that allow people to breathe. The vertebrae that make up the spine protect the spinal cord, the bundle of nerves responsible for carrying signals between the brain and the rest of the body.

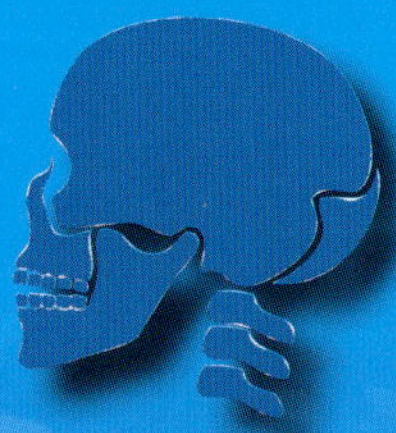

The skull is a set of fused bones that form a hard shell over the brain. The soft brain is vital because it is the body's control centre.

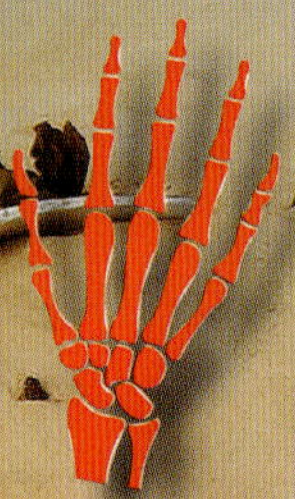

Bones are very tough, but they can still break. When a bone breaks it hurts because bones are partly made up of living cells and contain nerves. To see exactly how and where a bone is broken, doctors use x-rays. If the broken ends of the bone are held together, they can heal.

Get smart!

To help a broken bone heal neatly in an arm or leg, doctors usually keep it straight with a splint, or cover the area in a plaster cast that sets hard. These hold the bones still, even when the patient is moving around, for a month or two, until the bones mend. This helps the bone heal quickly and in the correct shape.

Skeletons are formed from hard bones so they are left behind long after the flesh of a dead animal has rotted away.

Bone produces new cells and blood vessels to close up the gap caused by a break.

Get flow chart smart!

How bones mend

Follow this flow chart to learn how a broken bone heals.

When an arm bone breaks, a doctor takes an X-ray image to see exactly how and where it is damaged.

The cast stays on for up to two months, holding the bone still, to help it heal more quickly and in the correct position.

To help the bone heal, the doctor covers the area in a plaster cast that sets hard. This holds the broken ends together.

The bone produces a lot of new cells and blood vessels to close up the gap caused by the break.

Flowchart Smart

Chapter 3

Joints

Bones are hard and rigid. Joints are the places where a bone connects to another bone so the skeleton can move. Three of the main joint types found in the body are hinge, ball-and-socket and pivot joints.

Hinge joints allow movement in one direction only, such as in the knees and elbows. They work in a similar way to the hinges on a door. There are small hinge joints in our fingers and toes, too.

To do the butterfly stroke, swimmers use the shoulder ball-and-socket joints to rotate their arms.

The ball-and-socket joints in a shoulder or hip allow those parts to move back and forth, sideways and to rotate. A ball-and-socket joint allows movement in all directions because it consists of one bone with a rounded end that sits inside a cup-shaped area at the end of another bone. The ball can swivel within the space of the cup so arms can rotate.

In a pivot joint, the moving bone rotates within a ring that is formed from a second bone. A pivot joint allows one bone to rotate around another. There is a pivot joint at the top of the spine. It allows the head to turn from side to side.

Get smart!

Some people can bend their fingers or arms in ways that most of us cannot. Although these people are often said to be double-jointed, this name is not really accurate. They do not have twice as many joints as other people. It is just that their ligaments, the band of fibres that connect bones at a joint, are more elastic, so stretch more than they do in other people.

Without joints, movements such as this would be impossible.

Other joints

Some joints in the body only allow for a little movement between bones. Other joints do not allow any movement at all!

Gliding joints occur between the surfaces of two flat bones that are held together by ligaments. Some of the bones in the wrists, ankles and spine move by gliding or sliding against each other. A hand waving from side to side is one example of the use of gliding joints.

Gliding joints allow bones that meet at flat surfaces, such as those in the spine, to glide past one another in any direction along the joint. This helps us bend, twist and sway.

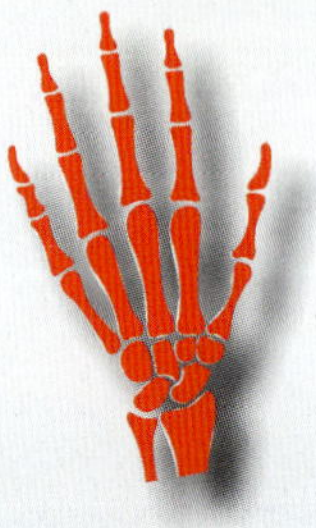

Joints that do not move are called immovable joints. There are fixed or immovable joints in the skull. When a baby is born, the bones that make up the skull are not fused together in a hard shell as they are in adults. This means the skull can be flexible and change shape slightly when the baby is born and squeezes through the mother's birth canal. After the baby is born, the parts of the skull fuse together into solid bone. The bony plates that make up a skull fit together like a jigsaw puzzle, linked by joins or joints, of fibrous tissue. Fibrous joints also hold the teeth in the jawbone.

Your spinal joints are covered with cartilage, which protects your bones from **friction** as you move.

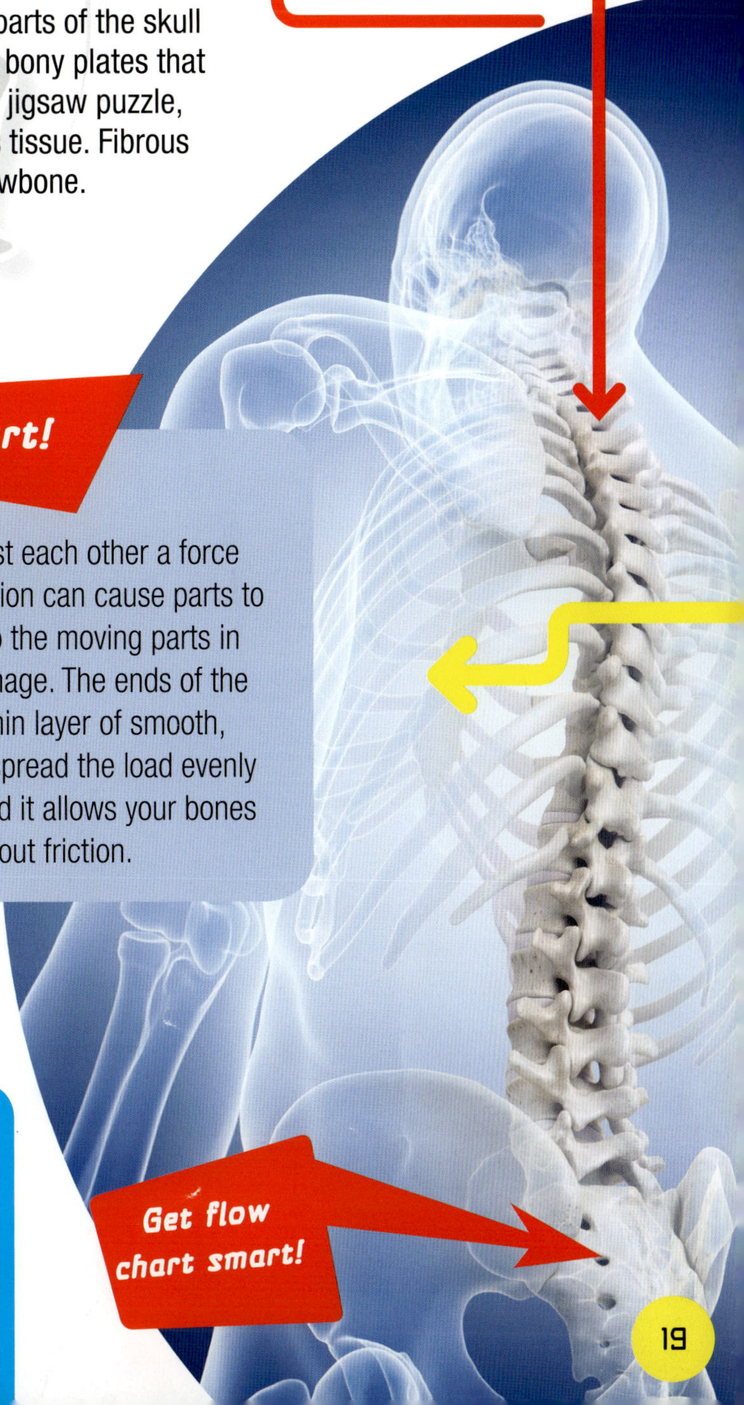

Get smart!

When two parts move against each other a force called **friction** is at work. Friction can cause parts to wear down. People add oil to the moving parts in machines to prevent this damage. The ends of the bones are covered with a thin layer of smooth, slippery cartilage. This helps spread the load evenly when pressure is put on it, and it allows your bones to move freely, without friction.

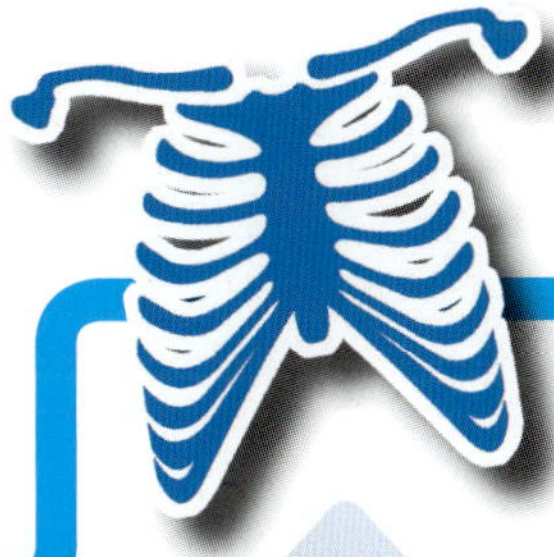

Get flow chart smart!

How joints work

This flow chart explains how bones move at joints.

A muscle pulls on a bone.

The bone is connected to the next bone by ligaments.

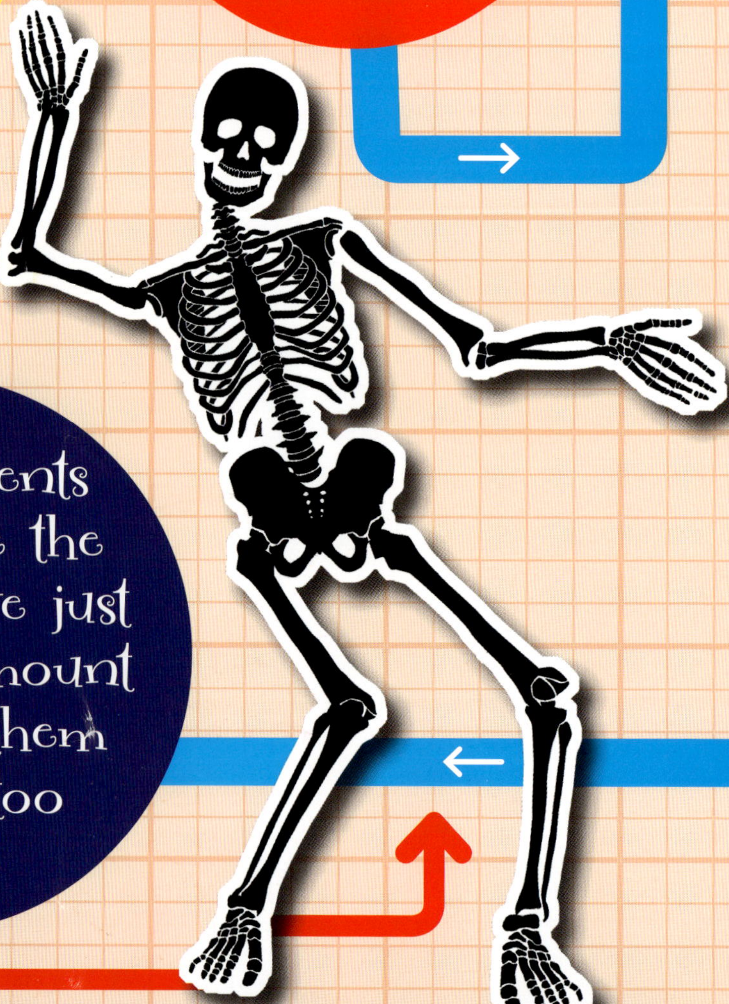

The ligaments make sure the bones move just the right amount and stop them moving too much.

The ligaments move and make the joint bend, straighten, or rotate.

Cartilage at the ends of the bones has a smooth, slippery surface to prevent bones scraping each other.

Flowchart Smart

Chapter 4
Muscles

Most of the muscles in the human body are attached to bones. These skeletal muscles are masses of strong, elastic tissue. Skeletal muscles are responsible for many different movements such as running, smiling, waving and weightlifting.

Muscles are made of fibres. Each fibre is made up of long, thin cells that are packed in bundles and wrapped in a thin skin. Each muscle has lots of bundles. Skeletal muscles come in different shapes and sizes, and consist of different arrangements of muscle fibres. There are very tiny strands of muscle in the ear and very large muscles in the thigh.

Strong muscles are not only found in legs and arms. The jaw muscle that moves the mouth is one of the strongest in the body.

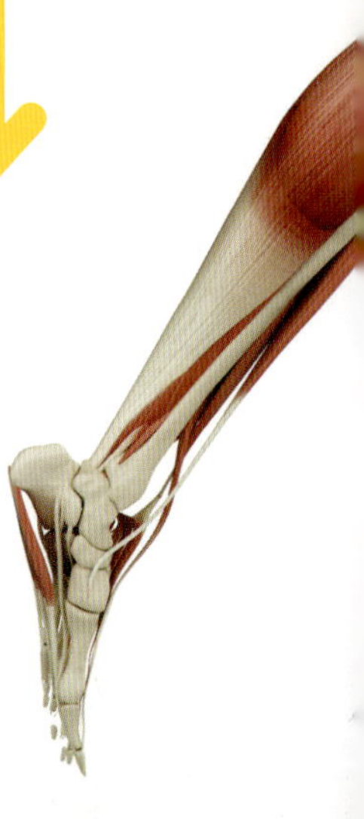

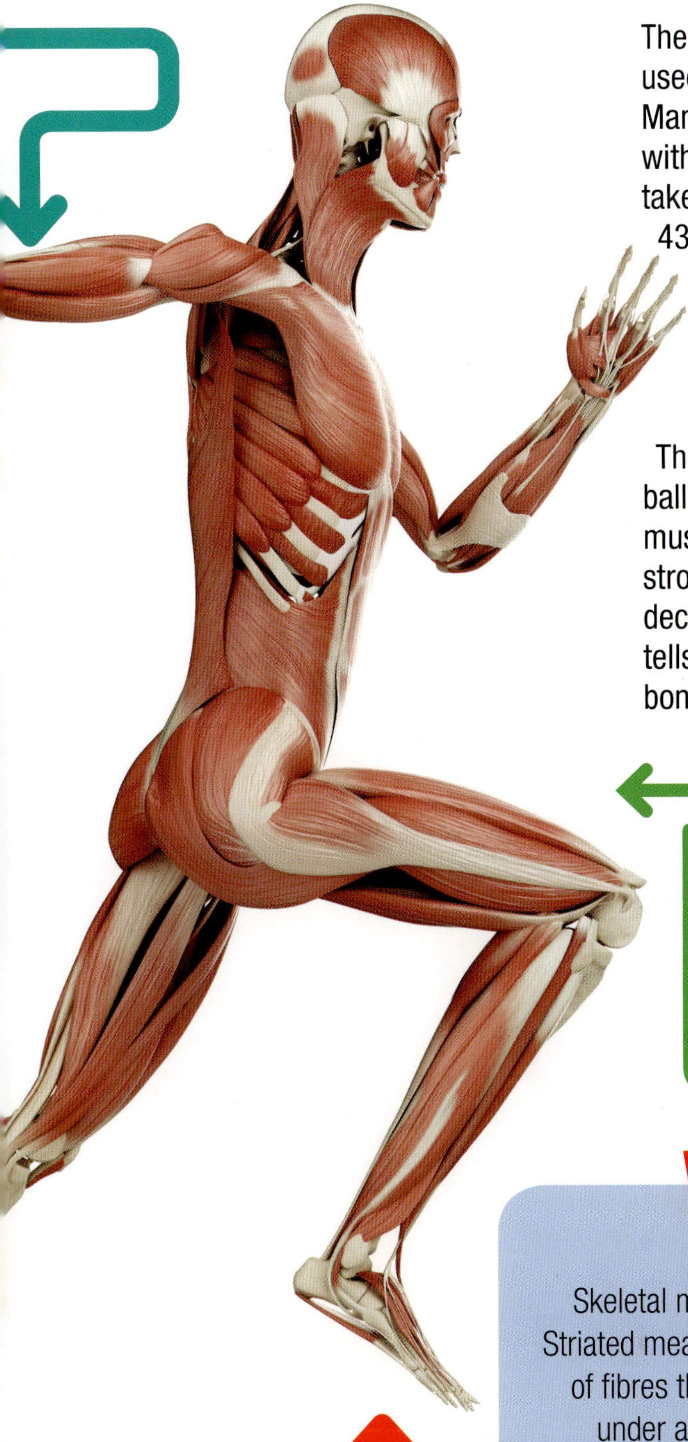

The chest has large, fan-shaped muscles, used to help pull arms and shoulders forward. Many different muscles help with different movements. For example, it takes 17 muscles in the face to smile and 43 muscles to frown!

Skeletal muscles are voluntary muscles, which means they only move when people want them to. The leg muscles only lift the leg to kick a ball when we want it to. The arm and hand muscles only move to allow someone to stroke a cat when they want to. The person decides to make a movement and the brain tells the muscles to work and move the bones necessary for that movement.

There are thousands of muscle fibres in every skeletal muscle. Bigger muscles have more bundles of fibres than smaller muscles.

Get smart!

Skeletal muscles are also called striated muscles. Striated means striped. Skeletal muscles are made up of fibres that have horizontal stripes when viewed under a microscope. The fibres look long and thin, and they are crossed with a regular pattern of fine red and white lines.

Other muscles

Skeletal muscles move the bones in the body and make up the majority of the body's muscles but there are also two other types of muscles. Smooth muscles and cardiac muscles work automatically without people having to think about them.

Smooth muscle is made of fibres that look smooth, not striped. Smooth muscles are found in body organs such as the stomach. Smooth muscles squeeze the walls of the stomach to help it break down food. There are also smooth muscles in the blood vessels and **intestines**. They squeeze the walls of the blood vessels so the blood inside keeps flowing around the body properly. Smooth muscles inside the walls of the intestine help keep food moving through the **digestive** system.

The bulk of a human heart is cardiac muscle. It works harder than any other muscle in the body.

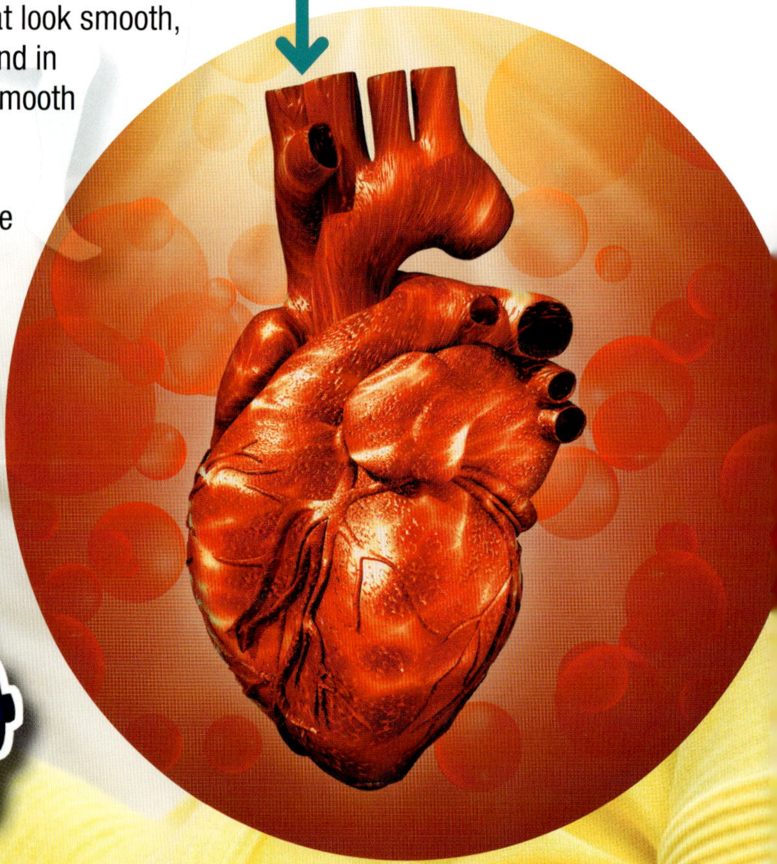

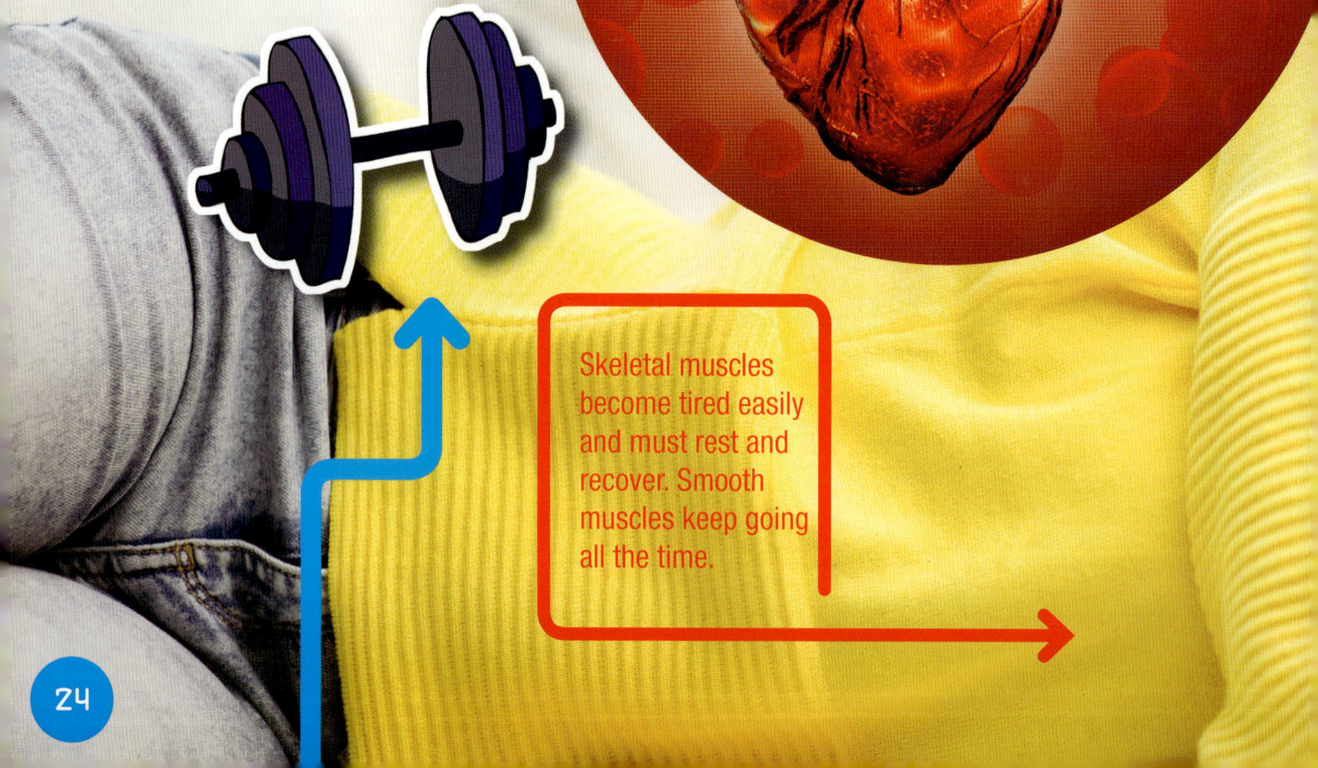

Skeletal muscles become tired easily and must rest and recover. Smooth muscles keep going all the time.

Get smart!

Involuntary muscles keep doing their job automatically even when people are asleep. This is important because it ensures the heart keeps beating all the time.

Cardiac muscle is found only in the heart. The walls of the heart are mostly made up of muscle fibres. Cardiac muscle squeezes the chambers of the heart to make the heart pump out blood with enough force that it travels all the way around the body. It also works automatically in a regular rhythm (beat) which can be felt at **pulse points** at the wrist or in the neck.

Muscle power

Muscles get the power they need from food. Muscle cells use digested food to get **energy**. They use this energy to grow and function.

Food is the body's fuel. When people eat, the food is swallowed and it passes into the stomach and intestines, where it is digested.

Get smart!

When athletes reach the end of a race their heart is beating faster than usual, they are panting and they are breathing hard. That is because their muscles have been working so hard that they have used up the glucose and oxygen available to them and need more. By breathing harder, the body increases the amount of oxygen it takes in and the heart beats faster to deliver more blood to the busy muscles.

After a hard workout or long race, muscles feel tired. Athletes need to sit down because their muscles have run out of energy.

The food is broken down into tiny pieces, including particles of glucose (sugar) which are small enough to enter the bloodstream. The heart pumps the blood around the body so that it can deliver glucose to the body's cells. All cells need glucose for energy.

As well as glucose, blood carries oxygen to the cells. Oxygen is a gas in the air. It enters the body when people breathe air into their lungs. Oxygen passes from the lungs into the blood. It travels to cells around the body. There are blood vessels in the muscles to carry oxygen and glucose to the muscle cells. In the muscle cells, glucose and oxygen combine and release energy.

All engines need a source of energy. Cars and other vehicles use fuel such as petrol. The human body and its muscles rely on food for fuel to make them work.

Get flow chart smart!

How muscles get energy

Follow the steps in this flow chart to see how muscles get the energy they need to work.

A person eats food and breathes in air.

The food is digested in the stomach and intestines. The air enters the lungs.

Tiny particles from the food enter the blood. In the lungs, oxygen from the air passes into the blood.

The blood carries the glucose particles and oxygen to the cells around the body.

When blood carrying oxygen and glucose reaches blood vessels in the muscles, muscle cells combine the glucose and the oxygen to release energy so they can work.

Flowchart Smart

Chapter 5

How muscles work

Muscles move bones and other parts of the body by pulling on them. Muscles cannot push on bones, they can only pull them. That is why most muscles work in pairs.

Muscles pull on bones by **contracting** (becoming shorter). As they get shorter, they pull on the bone to which they are attached. They also feel harder as they get shorter. If you put your hand on your upper arm and then bend the arm, you should be able to feel the muscles getting firmer. The problem is that after a muscle has pulled the bones, it cannot push them back to their original position.

Muscles work in pairs so that when a second muscle contracts, to pull the bones in the opposite direction, the first muscle relaxes. It gets longer and softer again. For example, the elbow joint has two muscles that move the forearm up or down. These are the biceps muscle on the front of the upper arm and the triceps at the back of the upper arm. When someone bends their arm at the elbow, the biceps contracts and the triceps relaxes. When they want to straighten the arm, the triceps contracts and the biceps relaxes.

Try lifting a heavy object like this and feel both your biceps and triceps muscle as you do so.

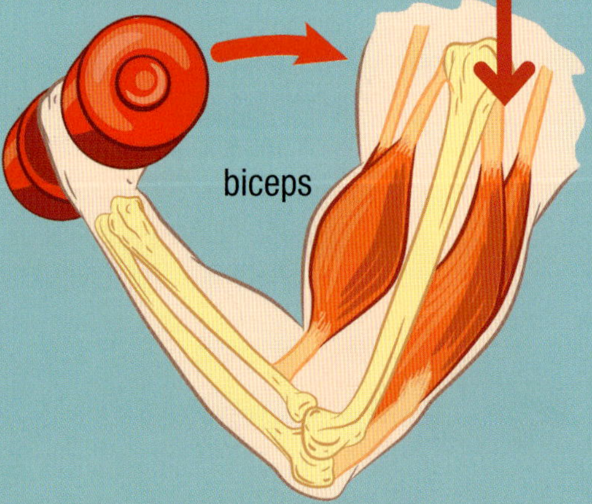

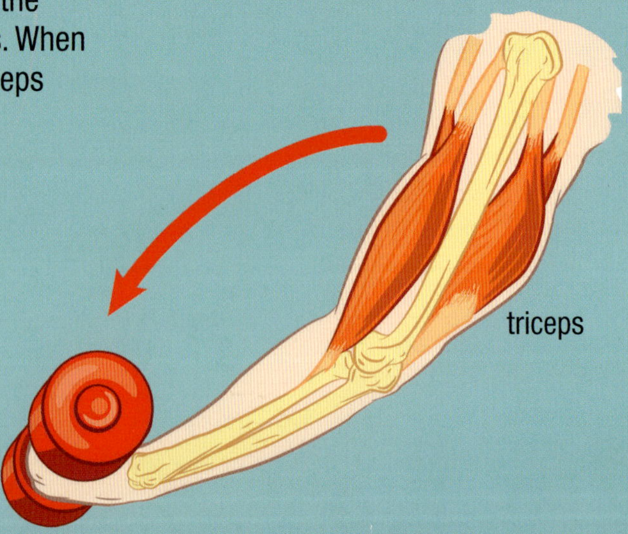

Get smart!

Muscle fibres can be overstretched if people contract them too suddenly or too hard. This is what people mean when they say they have "pulled" a muscle. Doctors call it muscle strain. Muscle strain can be very painful and stop the muscle working well for a while.

Strains can happen if people use the same muscle too much and for too long, or if someone suddenly lifts a weight that is heavier than they can manage.

Tendons

Muscles are attached to bones by strong **tendons**. Tendons are tough bands of cord-like **tissue**. They behave a bit like thick elastic bands. Tendons get tighter when a muscle contracts.

Tendons help people carry out large movements, such as jumping and running, and also delicate movements such as wiggling toes or fingers. If you wiggle your fingers, you can see the tendons on the back of your hand move as they work.

The easiest tendon to see in the body is the Achilles tendon. This is found at the back of the ankle. It connects the muscles in the calf of the leg to the heel bone. When the calf muscles contract, the Achilles tendon tightens and pulls the heel bone up. The Achilles tendon is what allows people to stand on tiptoe. If tendons are damaged, movement is restricted. If the Achilles tendon is damaged it is difficult, or even impossible, to walk.

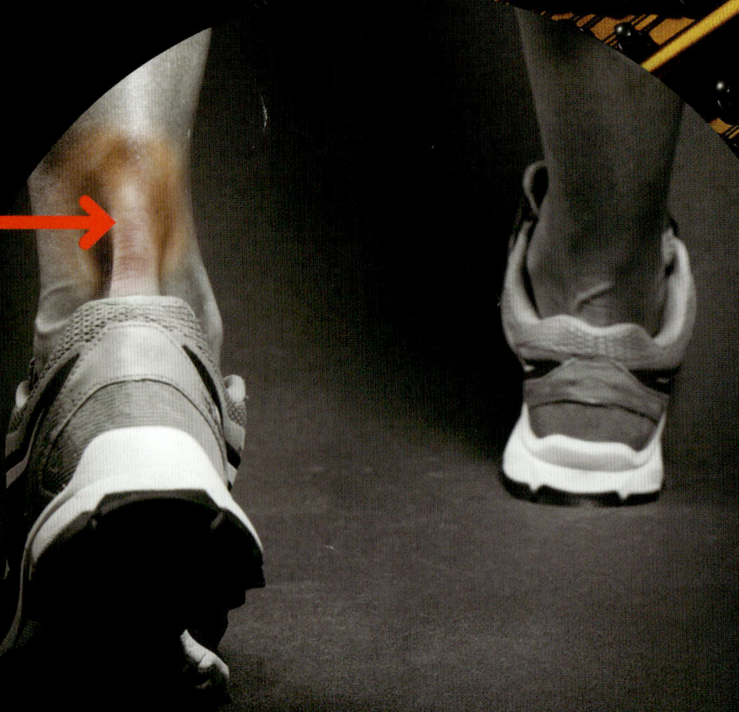

The Achilles tendon at the back of the foot is the thickest tendon in the human body and it is roughly 15 cm (6 inches) long.

Tendons in the hands and fingers are long. They slide back and forth by as much as 5 cm (2 inches) to make arms and fingers move.

Get smart!

The name Achilles tendon comes from an ancient Greek myth. The hero Achilles was incredibly strong because his mother had dipped him in a special river to make him invulnerable. Unfortunately his heel was not covered by the water so when a poisoned arrow struck him there as an adult, he died. If you hear someone say "that's their Achilles heel", they mean someone's vulnerability or point of weakness.

Controlling muscles

The muscles that are connected to and control the bones in the skeleton are voluntary. They move when the brain and the body's **nervous system** tells them to.

The brain is the body's control centre. It processes the information that it receives from the senses of touch, sight, hearing, taste and smell about the body's surroundings. It makes decisions about how the body should respond. Then the brain sends messages along a system of nerves to the muscles, telling them how to move. There are nerves inside the muscles, too, which receive the instructions.

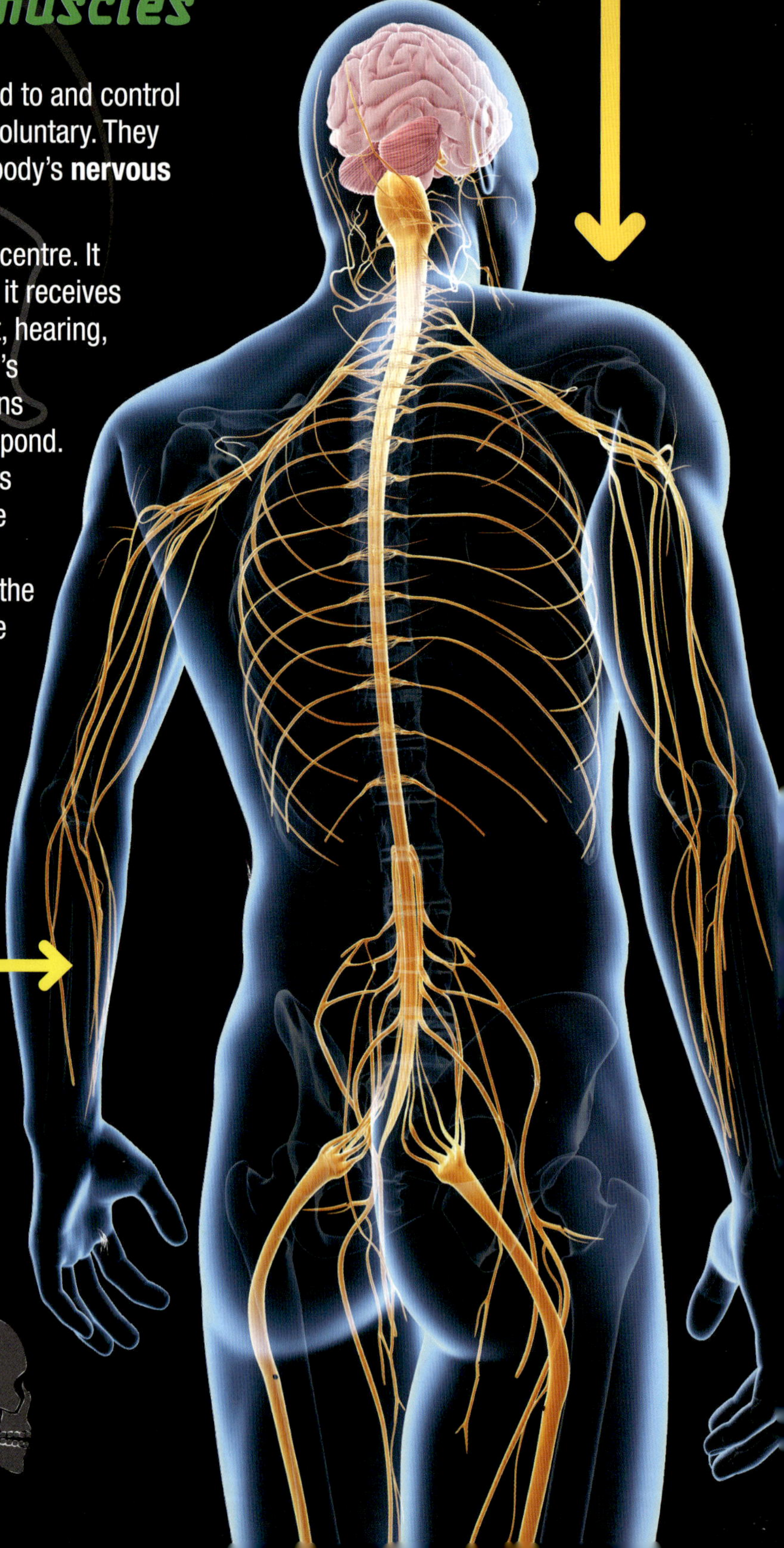

The nervous system is the collection of nerves that run through the body connecting other parts of the body to the brain, its control centre.

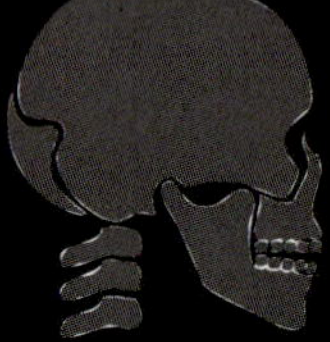

Get smart!

The involuntary muscles, which control activities such as breathing, swallowing, **blood pressure** and the heartbeat, are run by structures deep within the brain and the upper part of the spinal cord. This area is called the **brain stem**.

The voluntary muscles are controlled by the parts of the brain known as the motor cortex, a small area on the outer part of the brain, and the cerebellum, a part found at the back of the brain. When you decide to move, the motor cortex sends a signal, called a nerve impulse, through the spinal cord and along the nerves to the muscles, telling them to contract.

As a body part such as an arm or leg moves, nerve impulses from the **joints** and muscles are sent along nerves to the cerebellum. They tell the cerebellum where and how the arm or leg is moving and what position it is in. Then the cerebellum sends more messages to the muscles to make sure the movements are coordinated and run smoothly.

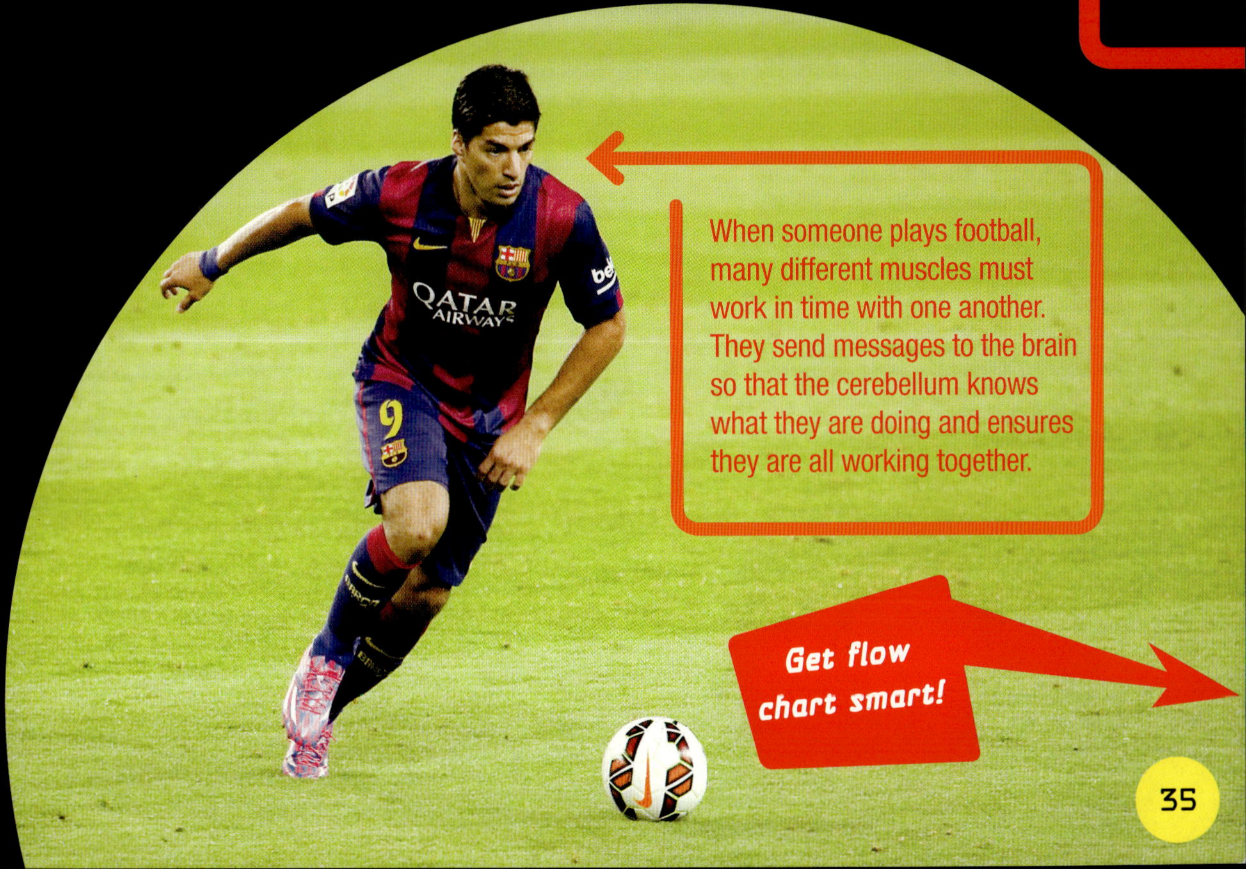

When someone plays football, many different muscles must work in time with one another. They send messages to the brain so that the cerebellum knows what they are doing and ensures they are all working together.

Get flow chart smart!

Voluntary movements

This flow chart follows the steps that happen when muscles bend and straighten an arm.

A person wants to bend his arm.

A message travels from the brain, via nerves, to the muscles in the arm.

This makes the biceps muscle relax.

The biceps muscle on the front of the upper arm contracts and shortens.

→

This pulls on the tendon that connects the muscle to the elbow joint. The arm bends at the elbow.

↓

When he wants to drop his arm down again, he contracts his triceps muscle.

←

This pulls on the tendon that connects the triceps to the elbow joint. The arm straightens.

Flowchart Smart

Chapter 6

Taking care of muscles and bones

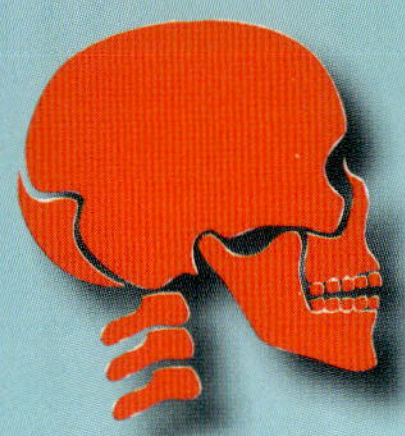

The human body uses food as fuel and to get the substances it needs to build healthy muscles and bones. That is why one of the ways to care for muscles and bones is to eat well.

Bones stop growing when people are about 20 years old, but bone cells keep on working. They repair bones if they break and they maintain the strength and health of the bones. Bones are partly made up of calcium so it is important to eat a diet that contains calcium. Dairy foods such as milk, cheese and yogurt are rich in calcium, as are bony fish such as sardines, and green leafy vegetables such as spinach, beans, nuts and seeds. Other body parts require calcium, too, such as teeth, and nerves and muscles need calcium to work properly. Bones use some calcium and store some so they can release it into the blood when it is needed elsewhere.

The bulk of muscle tissue is made up of **proteins**, so eating a diet that contains protein is important. The body needs protein to build healthy muscles, to repair muscle fibres when they are damaged and to make new fibres when old ones wear out. Proteins are found in foods such as meat, seafood, fish, eggs, beans and nuts.

Have a healthy, well-balanced diet and exercise every day. Eating fruit, vegetables, potatoes, pasta and bread will give you the glucose you need to fuel your muscles.

It is especially important for children to get enough calcium in their diet because the body is still building bones to help them grow.

Get smart!

To stay healthy and get the energy needed to live and grow, people must eat a balanced diet. That means eating one or two servings of protein a day, several servings of dairy foods and at least five servings of fruit and vegetables. We also need **carbohydrates** such as rice, bread or potatoes at most meals, and should only eat small amounts of fatty and sugary foods.

Exercise

It is important to get regular exercise to keep bones and muscles strong and working well. Exercise makes bones and muscles stronger.

Regular exercise gives muscles more stamina. This means muscles can keep working and moving for longer. It also means they are less likely to get muscle strain or other injuries. Exercise keeps bones strong and stops joints getting stiff. Doing a variety of activities exercises a variety of muscles and bones. For example, walking, running and cycling are good for leg muscles, and rowing and tennis are good for arm muscles. **Weight-bearing** exercises such as tennis, running, walking and dancing are great for bones, too.

Warm-ups are gentle exercises that people do before exercise or sport. These include light jogging, knee bends and stretches. They prepare muscles and joints for activity so there is less chance of straining a muscle, tendon or **ligament**. When someone does a warm-up routine, their heart beats faster. This increases blood flow to the muscles, giving them more oxygen and glucose. This gives the muscles more energy and warms them, which helps them react more quickly. Warm-ups also increase blood flow and temperature in the joints, loosening them up and giving them a greater range of movement.

The best exercise for your body, your muscles and your bones is one that you enjoy, because if you enjoy it you are likely to do it more often!

Get smart!

Do muscles have a memory? In a way they do! When people repeat a particular muscle movement again and again, the muscles being used remember that action and become more precise in what they do. That is why practice is very important when learning a sport.

Get flow chart smart!

Doing 10–15 minutes of gentle exercise and stretching before sport warms muscles, which helps prevent muscle strain.

Preparation for exercise

The steps in this flow chart show how warm-ups help the body get ready for sport and exercise.

A person spends 15 minutes slow jogging, stretching and bending before a football match.

Having more energy allows the muscles to react quicker. The muscles are ready to make bigger, faster movements when the match begins.

Warm-ups also warm and loosen the joints, giving them a greater range of movement.

The warm-up makes their heart beat faster, increasing the flow of blood around the body.

The increased blood flow to the muscles provides them with more oxygen and glucose.

Muscle cells use the glucose and oxygen to release more energy.

As muscle cells release more energy, the muscles become warmer.

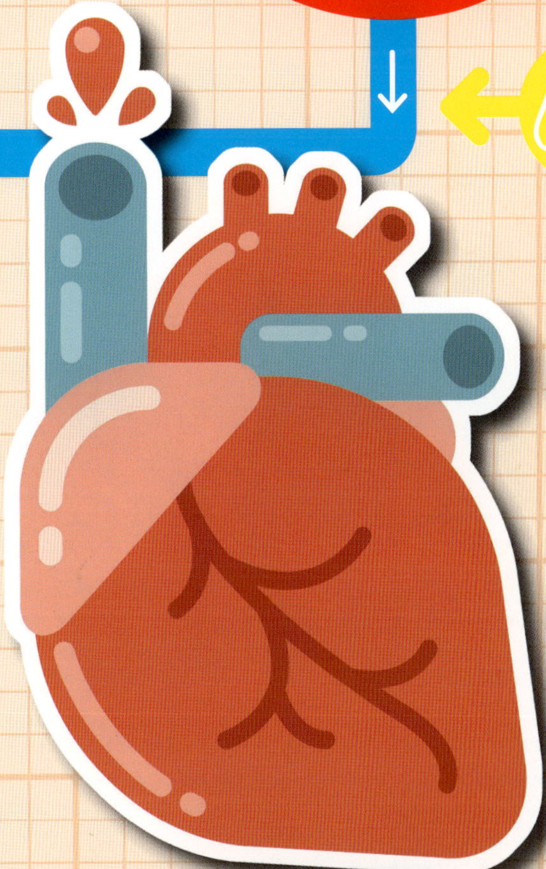

Flowchart Smart

Play it safe

It is important to take proper care of bones and muscles by having the right equipment when doing sport and exercise. Accidents happen, but taking precautions can prevent broken bones and bruised muscles.

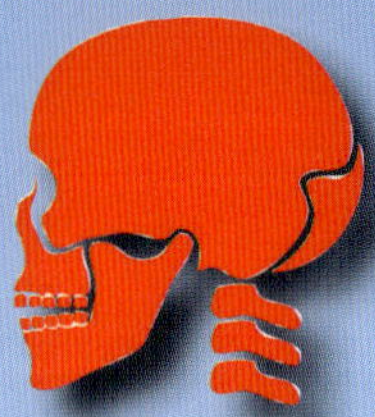

When running, doing gymnastics, playing football or doing any type of activity where you might trip or fall over, it is very important to wear shoes that grip the surface well. This can help prevent broken bones, damaged joints and bruised muscles. For activities such as skateboarding, cycling or roller-skating, it is best to wear a helmet and knee and elbow pads. These cover bones and joints in padding and protect them from damage.

Wearing protective clothing can prevent bones being broken and muscles being bruised and injured.

The bones and muscles in our body support us and help us move every day in many different ways. They cover **organs** and other parts inside the body to ensure these do not get damaged. They keep our bodies healthy and working efficiently. It is our job to take care of our bones and muscles, so they can continue to take care of us!

The skull is made up of tough bones and it does a good job of protecting your brain. The skull can be damaged, however, in a fall from a skateboard or bike. Always wear a helmet!

Get smart!

Taking care of your bones when you are young can help you stay strong and healthy when you are older. When people get to the age of 30, they begin to lose bone density. Their bones become gradually thinner and weaker as they naturally lose some calcium. By building strong bones in your youth, you can slow down the weakening process as you age.

Glossary

blood pressure force that the heart uses to pump blood around the body

blood vessels tubes that carry blood around the body

brain body's control centre

brain stem part of the brain that controls the flow of messages between the brain and the rest of the body

calcium mineral that gives bones their strength

carbohydrates substances in foods that give the body energy to live and grow

cartilage smooth rubbery material

cells very small parts that together form all living things

collagen strong, slightly stretchy substance that helps form bones

contracting becoming shorter

digestive to do with the breakdown of food so the body can use it

energy capacity to do work

friction force that causes resistance when two surfaces rub together

intestines tube running from the stomach to the anus

joints places where two bones meet

ligaments bands of fibres that connect bones to other bones

minerals non-living natural substances such as sand, salt or calcium

nerves fibres that carry messages between the brain and the rest of the body

nervous system system of nerves in the body that sends messages between the brain and the other parts of the body

organs body parts such as the heart or liver

oxygen gas in the air

pelvis ring of bones to which the leg bones are attached

proteins substances in some foods that the body uses to build or repair body parts

pulse points places on the body where you can feel the rate of the heartbeat

spinal cord bundle of nerves inside the spine, which run from the brain down the back

spine backbone

tendons tough, cord-like fibres that attach muscles to bones

tissue group of cells of the same type that do a job together, for example, muscle cells form muscle tissue

vertebrae set of bones that link together to form the spine (backbone)

weight-bearing describes an activity in which the body supports its own weight

Find out more

Books

Human Body: A Visual Encyclopedia, DK (DK Publishing, 2018)

Understanding Our Skeleton (Brains, Body, Bones!), Lucy Beevor (Raintree, 2017)

Your Skin and Bones: Understand them with Numbers (Your Body by Numbers), Melanie Waldron (Raintree, 2014)

Your Physical Body: From Birth to Old Age (Your Body for Life), Anne Rooney (Raintree, 2014)

Websites

Discover more about what your skeleton does at:
www.bbc.co.uk/guides/zqfdpbk

Find out more about your skeleton at:
www.dkfindout.com/uk/human-body/skeleton-and-bones/

Find out more about your muscles at:
www.dkfindout.com/uk/human-body/muscles/

Index